Learn to Hand Sew for Mini Dolls

A Beginner's Guide to Sewing for Mini Dolls

Sherralyn St. Clair

COPYRIGHT

Copyright 2018 Sherralyn St. Clair

You may sell or give away any of the doll clothing you make yourself. The clothing cannot be mass produced without my permission. You may make as many copies of the patterns as you need for your own use. You may not give away or sell the patterns or the instructions, or kits containing the patterns or instructions. If you plan to use this book for a project with a scout, church, or other community group, please email me at sherralyn@sherralynsdolls.com for permission to make a copy of the patterns for each student. If this book is used in a for-profit setting, each student should purchase a copy of the book.

Version 09/30/18

ISBN-13: 978-1726078092

ISBN-10: 1726078094

Introduction

The patterns in the book will fit 6½" American Girl® mini dolls; Our Generation® mini dolls and Lori mini dolls from Target®; Madame Alexander® Travel Friends dolls; and my Twinkle mini doll.

This book was written at the request of some of my readers. I was surprised at the number of people who wanted to use mini doll clothes patterns to teach a child to sew. My pattern book *Sewing for Mini Dolls* was written for intermediate sewers, not beginners and these readers were disappointed.

Learn to Hand Sew for your Doll is designed for beginning sewers, but it is not written specifically as a children's book. The patterns are extremely easy, but children who use the book will still need adult help. An adult should explain the instructions and pattern markings and help cut out the project pieces. The last three projects (visor, sandals, and bear) will require adult help.

The patterns are designed for four-way stretch knits. They are intended for handsewing. An experienced sewer may sew these patterns with a machine. I recommend using a zigzag stitch and wash away stabilizer. Children just learning to sew should use handsewing to make the projects.

Most of the doll models in this book are Our Generation® mini dolls and Lori mini dolls from Target®. The slightly taller doll with jointed knees is a Madame Alexander® Travel Friends doll. The cloth dolls are my Twinkle mini dolls. The horse, dogs, and motor scooter are from Target's Lori series. The plastic and leatherette shoes came with some of the mini dolls in my collection. The sneakers, felt shoes, and felt mouse slippers came from patterns in my book, *Sewing for Mini Dolls*. That book also has patterns for the socks and tights that some of the dolls shown here are wearing.

Table of Contents

Get Started..........................4

Learn Sewing Skills................7

Nightgown, Dress, or Shirt......10

Swimsuit..........................12

Beach Robe or Robe................14

Vest..............................16

Skirt.............................18

Sleeveless Dress or Top...........20

Jumper............................22

Sundress..........................24

Jacket............................26

Visor, Sandals, and Bear.........28

Patterns..........................33

More Books.......................39

Spoonflower......................40

Get Started

Gather Your Sewing Tools

Scissors

Sharp scissors a little smaller than dressmaking scissors are a good choice for these projects. I use Singer, 6½" (16.5 cm) sewing scissors with pink and white comfort grip and Scotch Precision Scissors, 6" (15 cm).

Pins

I usually use glass head silk pins. Some people may prefer the smaller metal headed pins for these small projects. A pin cushion keeps your pins from getting lost.

Needles

I recommend a size 8 embroidery needle, because it has a large eye that is easy to thread. As the number of the needle size becomes larger, the needle itself becomes smaller. Size 7 needles have larger eyes and shafts than size 8 needles. Size 9 needles have smaller eyes and shafts than size 8 needles.

Needle Threader

You can use a needle threader if you like. Learn how to use it on p. 7.

Thimble

I always use a thimble for hand sewing, but many people do not. Try it to see if you like it. Learn how to use it on p. 8.

Ruler

You will need a small (6" or 150 mm) ruler.

Safety pin

You need a small safety pin to put elastic in the doll's skirt. You can use a sewing bodkin instead, if you have one.

Gather Your Supplies

Four-way Stretch Knits

All of the clothing must be made from four-way stretch knit fabric. **Woven fabric will not work for these patterns.** The knit does not ravel and so will not need hemming. It will stretch enough to dress the doll without the need for snaps or hook and loop tape. You can use scraps of four-way stretch knit, including old tights and leggings. You can buy remnants and quarter yards of four-way stretch knits.

You can also buy a fat quarter of knit from Spoonflower® that has all the clothing printed on it. Just cut each piece out and sew it together. See p. 40.

Felt

Use felt scraps in the color of your choice for the sandals' soles, if you like. A gray or black color works well for the bottom sole.

You may use felt or knit fabric for the bear.

Card Stock

You will need an index card or other card stock for the visor. You can use an index card instead of felt for the sandals' soles.

Thread

I think that cotton embroidery floss works best for handsewing, because it is strong and does not tangle as easily as synthetic threads. Embroidery floss is sold as a length of six threads twisted together. Learn how to separate one thread for sewing on p. 7.

You can use machine sewing thread, if you wish.

Elastic

Use ¼" (6 mm) elastic for the skirt and visor.

Glue

Use a tacky white glue for the sandals' felt soles and for gluing on the bear's eyes and nose.

Use the same tacky glue or Elmer's® X-treme glue stick for the visor and sandals with index card soles.

Black Glass Beads and Stuffing

For the bear you need two black 2 mm beads for the eyes and one ⅛" glass black bead for the nose. Use polyester fiberfill or a cotton ball that you have "fluffed up" to stuff the bear.

Doll

You will also need a 6½" (17 cm) doll to model your creations.

Learn Sewing Skills

To make the doll clothes in this book you need to know: how to thread a needle; how to sew the running stitch; how to use a thimble if you like; how to read a pattern; how to pin a pattern to fabric; how cut the fabric out; how to refold the fabric piece; and where to sew the piece together.

Prepare Your Embroidery Thread

If you are using embroidery floss, cut a length of floss about 24" (60 cm) long. Separate one piece of thread from the twisted floss. When you need to thread the needle again, separate another thread from the floss.

Thread a Needle

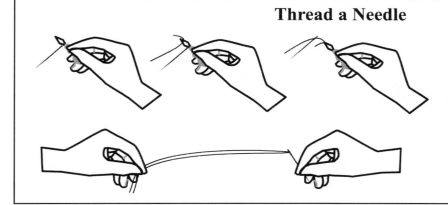

Poke the end of the thread through the needle's eye or use a needle threader as shown in the picture.

Pull the thread half way through the needle, so that the two ends line up.

Knot the Ends of Your Thread

Keep both ends of thread together and make a square knot.

Wrap the thread through the square knot circle three more times.

Pull the knot into a tight ball.

Trim the thread below the knot, but leave a short tail.

Sew the Running Stitch

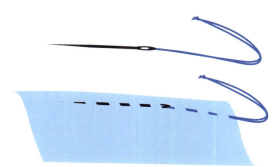

Sew the running stitch by going in and out of the fabrics you are joining with the threaded needle.

When you finish sewing the seam, sew over the last stitch four to five times to make sure that the seam will not come out. Then you can cut the thread.

Learn to use a Thimble

If you would like to use a thimble, hold the needle between your thumb and index finger. Put your thimble on your middle finger and push the needle through the fabric with the thimble.

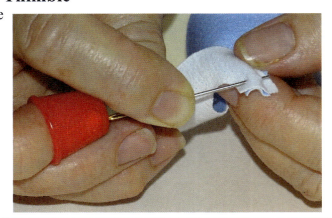

Learn to Read Patterns

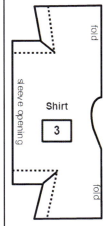

The patterns start on page p 33.

Copy them with a copier or trace each one as you need it. If you have a printer and would like a PDF file of the patterns, email me at sherralyn@sherralynsdolls.com and I will send the free PDF file to you.

Cut out your copy of the pattern that you need.

If the word "fold" is written next to the black line, that part of the pattern is pinned to the folded edge of the fabric.

The dashed lines on the pattern show where to sew the fabric together with the running stitch.

Cut Out the Pattern

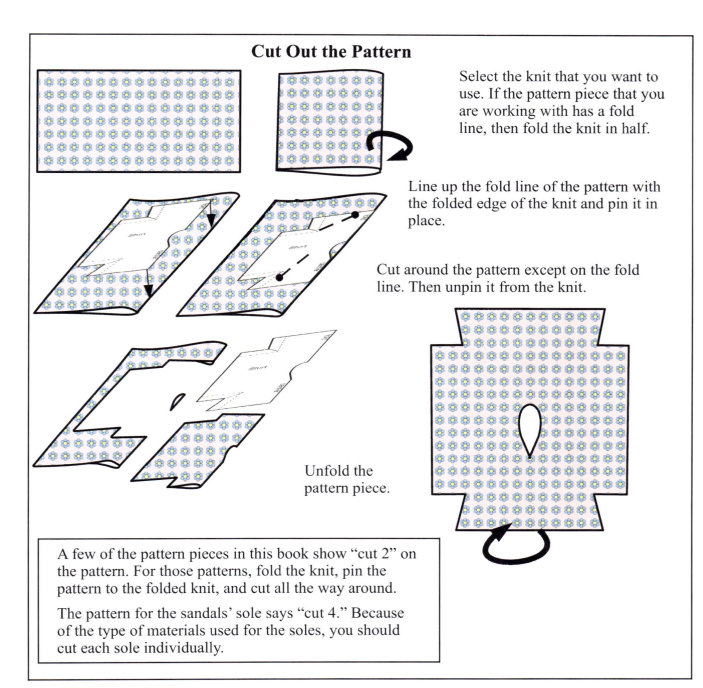

Select the knit that you want to use. If the pattern piece that you are working with has a fold line, then fold the knit in half.

Line up the fold line of the pattern with the folded edge of the knit and pin it in place.

Cut around the pattern except on the fold line. Then unpin it from the knit.

Unfold the pattern piece.

A few of the pattern pieces in this book show "cut 2" on the pattern. For those patterns, fold the knit, pin the pattern to the folded knit, and cut all the way around.

The pattern for the sandals' sole says "cut 4." Because of the type of materials used for the soles, you should cut each sole individually.

Sew up the Patterns

The rest of the instructions in this book show you how to fold and sew each piece that you have cut out. If you are using knits that you have selected, cut out a pattern from the book using the instructions on this page. If you are using the Spoonflower fat quarter, just cut around project you want to make. Use the Table of Contents to find the project you are working on and follow the directions to sew it up.

Nightgown, Dress, or Shirt

Cut out pattern 1, 2, or 3. If you are using the preprinted fabric from Spoonflower, cut out that piece. Open out the fabric piece, if you have cut it from a pattern.

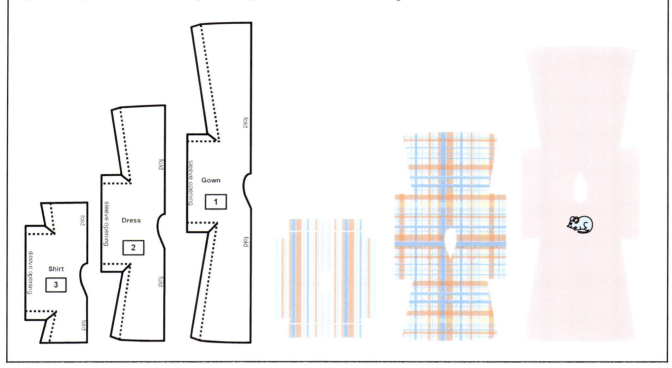

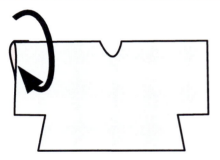

Fold the pattern piece as shown so that the right or printed side is on the inside.

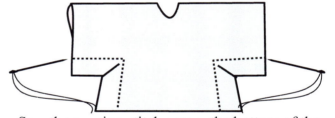

Sew the running stitch across the bottom of the sleeves and down the sides.

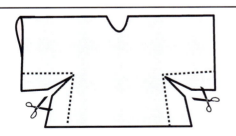

Clip between the sleeves and the sides. Be very careful not to cut the stitching thread.

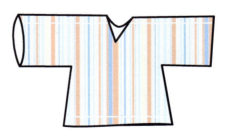

Turn right side out. If the doll has "big hair" she should "step into" the garment through the neck opening. Then slip her arms through the neck opening into the sleeves.

Swimsuit

Cut out pattern 4. Or if you are using the preprinted fabric from Spoonflower, cut out that piece. Open out the fabric piece, if you have cut it from a pattern.

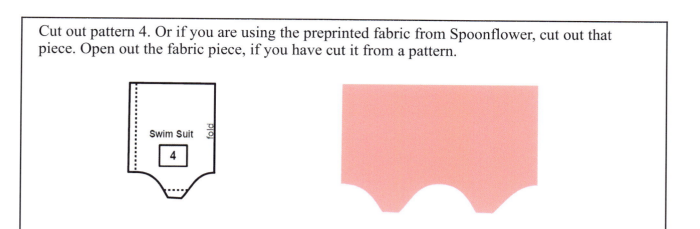

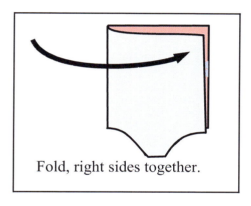

Fold, right sides together.

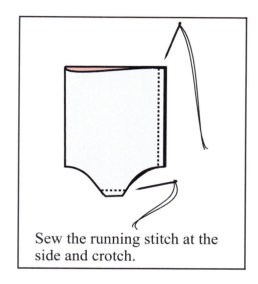

Sew the running stitch at the side and crotch.

Turn right side out. Help the doll "step into" her swimsuit.

Beach Robe or Robe

Cut out pattern 5 or 6. Or if you are using the preprinted fabric from Spoonflower, cut out that piece. Open out the fabric piece, if you have cut it from a pattern.

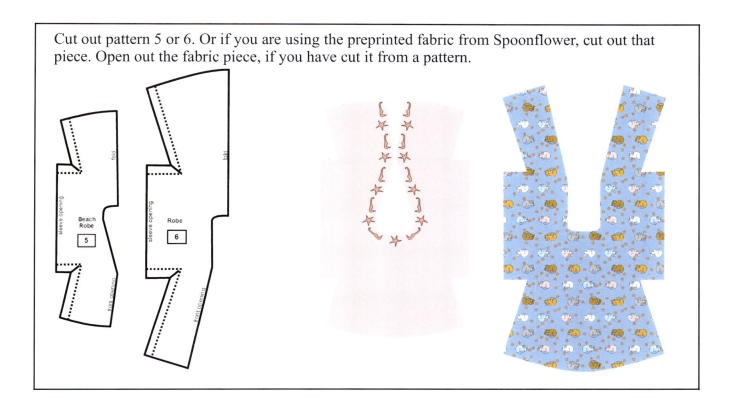

Fold, right or printed sides together.

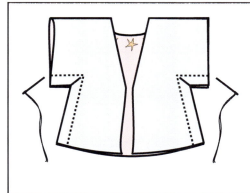

Sew the running stitch across the bottom of the sleeves and down the sides. Clip seams at the clip marks. Be careful not to cut stitches.

Turn right side out. Slip the doll's arms through the sleeves.

Vest

Cut out pattern 7. Or if you are using the preprinted fabric from Spoonflower, cut out that piece. Open out the fabric piece, if you have cut it from a pattern.

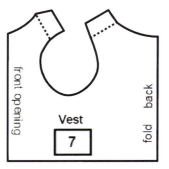

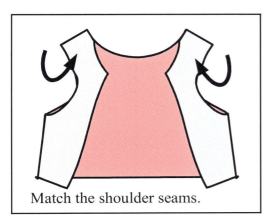

Match the shoulder seams.

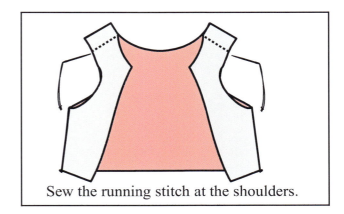

Sew the running stitch at the shoulders.

Turn right side out. Slip the doll's arms through the arm holes.

17

Skirt

Cut out pattern 8. Or if you are using the preprinted fabric from Spoonflower, cut out that piece. Open out the skirt if you have cut it from a pattern.

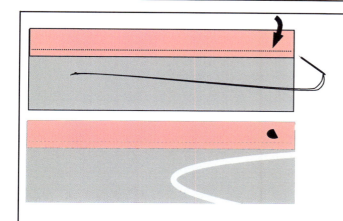

Fold the casing area to the back of the fabric. Sew the running stitch across the folded fabric to form a casing.

Attach the ⅛" (3mm) elastic to the safety pin. Use the pin to push the elastic through the casing that you have just made.

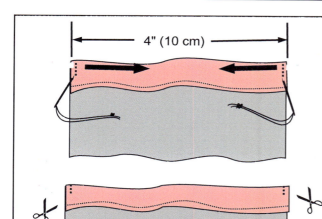

Gather the casing on the elastic until the casing is about 4" (10 cm) long. Try it on the doll's waist. Some of the Target dolls may need the elastic to be a little longer. Sew the elastic to the skirt at both ends.

Cut off the extra elastic.

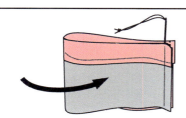

Fold the skirt in half, right sides together. Sew the ends together.

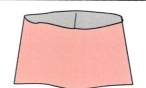

Turn the skirt right side out. Slip the doll's skirt over her feet and legs and onto her waist.

Sleeveless Dress or Top

Cut out pattern 8 or 9. Or if you are using the preprinted fabric from Spoonflower, cut out that piece. Open out the fabric piece, if you have cut it from a pattern.

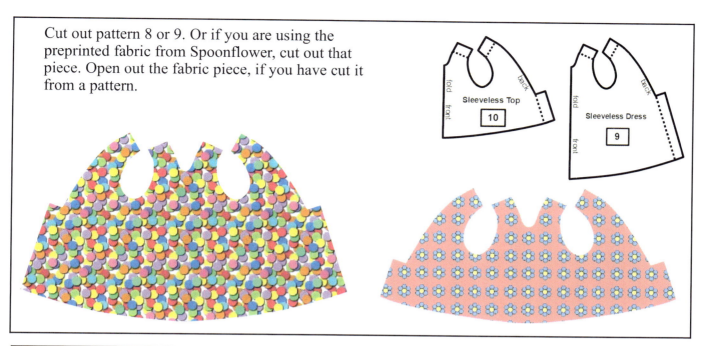

Match the shoulder seams.

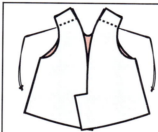
Sew the running stitch across the shoulder seams.

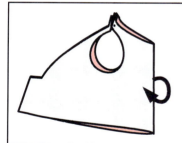
Refold so that the back lines are together.

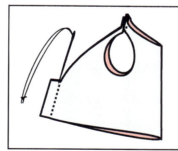
Sew the back seam.

Turn right side out. If the doll has "big hair" she should "step into" the garment through the neck opening. Then slip her arms through the neck opening into the arm holes.

Jumper

Cut out pattern 11. If you are using the preprinted fabric from Spoonflower, cut out that piece. Open out the fabric piece if you have cut it from a pattern.

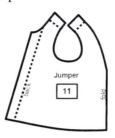

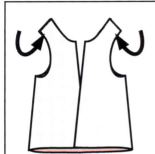
Match the shoulder seams.

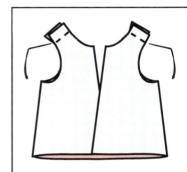
Sew the running stitch across the shoulder seams.

Refold so that the back lines are together.

Sew the back seam.

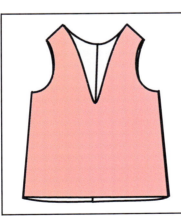
Turn right side out. First put on the doll's shirt. If the doll has "big hair" she should "step into" the garment through the neck opening. Then slip her arms and sleeves through the neck opening into the arm holes.

Sundress

Cut out patterns 12 and 13. Or if you are using the preprinted fabric from Spoonflower, cut out the pieces. Lay out the pieces.

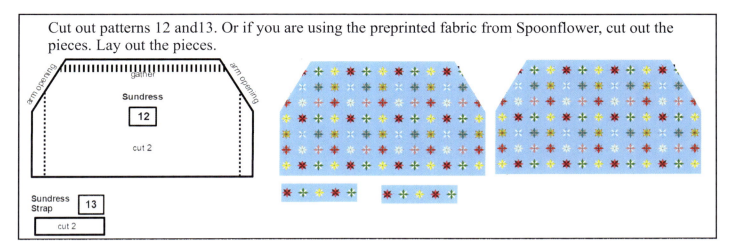

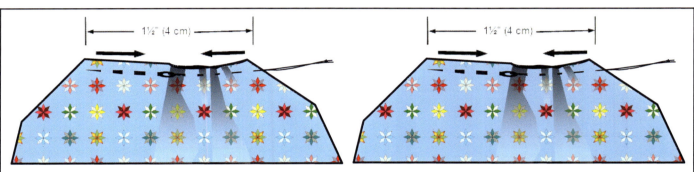

One of the two large pieces will be the front of the sundress and the other piece will be the back. Gather each of these pieces where the pattern indicates at the top of the dress. Hand gathering stitches are running stitches that are pulled so that the fabric is gathered over the thread. After you have sewn across the area at the top of each sundress piece, push the fabric on the sewing thread until the gathering is about 1½" (4 cm). Then sew the last stitch in the same spot four or five times as you did for a running stitch.

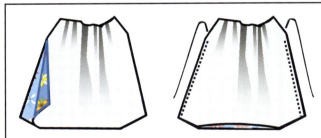

With the right sides together, sew the front and back together at the sides. Begin at the bottom of the arm openings as shown on the pattern.

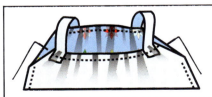

Sew shoulder straps at the arm hole openings.

Turn right side out. If the doll has "big hair" she should "step into" the garment through the neck opening between the straps. Then slip her arms through the arm openings.

25

Jacket

Cut out pattern 14. Or if you are using the preprinted fabric from Spoonflower, cut out that piece. Open out, if you have cut it from a pattern.

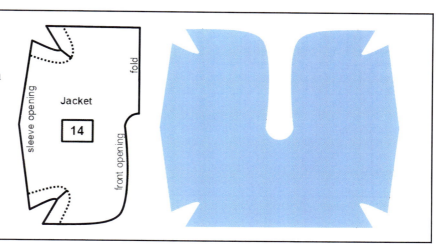

Fold the jacket in half with right sides touching.

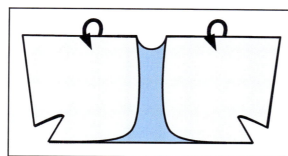

Sew the sleeve and side seams.

Clip the fabric at the clip marks. Be careful not to cut your stitches.

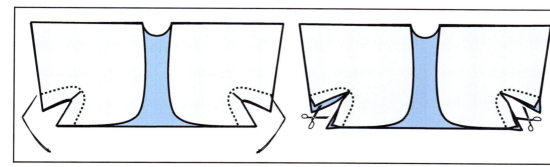

Turn the jacket right side out. Slip the doll's arms through the sleeves.

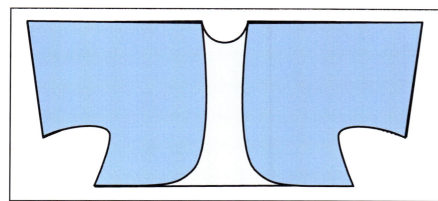

Visors, Sandals, and Bears

Making a Visor

Follow these steps when making a visor from a pattern. (Pattern piece 15)

Follow these steps when making a visor from Spoonflower knit.

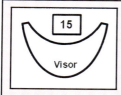 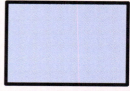 Cut out a 2" by ¾" (5×2 cm) rectangle from your chosen knit

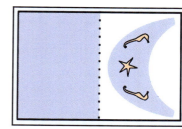 Cut out the rectangle that includes the two parts of the visor. Keep the two parts together on the rectangle

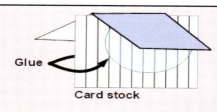 Fold the rectangle of knit in half wrong sides together. Place a piece of card stock between the folded knit. An index card works well. Glue the folded knit to both sides of the card.

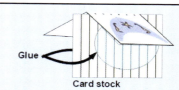 Fold the rectangle in half along the dotted line. Fold the unprinted sides of the knit against a piece of card stock. An index card works well. Glue the folded knit to both sides of the card.

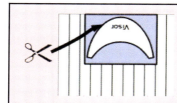 When the glue has dried, cut around the visor pattern.

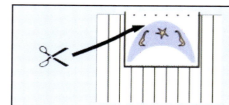 When the glue has dried, cut around the visor.

Now follow these steps for both pattern based and Spoonflower based visor designs.

 Sew elastic to one side of the visor.

 Fit the visor around your doll's head and sew the elastic to the other side of the visor.

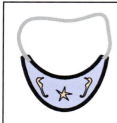 Outline the visor with craft paint or tacky glue. (Option)

Making Sandals

Follow these steps when making sandals from a pattern. (Pattern pieces 16 and 17)

Follow these steps when making sandals from Spoonflower knit.

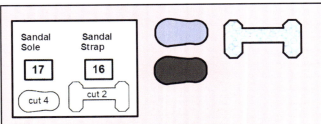

Cut out the sandal straps from four-way stretch knit. Cut two insoles and two soles from felt. For a thinner sole, you can use card stock.

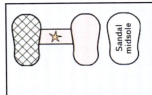

Cut out the sandal from the Spoonflower fat quarter. Use pattern piece 17 to cut out a Sandal midsole from felt. For a thinner sole, you can use card stock.

Lay the insole on the wrong side of the sandal strap, between the two strap anchors.

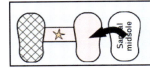

Glue the midsole to the colored side of insole.

Fold the first strap anchor and glue it to the back of the insole.

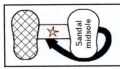

Fold the midsole under the strap.

Fold the second strap anchor and glue it on top of the first strap anchor.

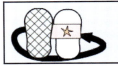

Fold the sole under the midsole and glue.

Glue the sole on top of the stack.

Check that the doll's foot fits under the strap. Allow the glue to dry.

Turn the sandal over. Check that the doll's foot fits under the strap. Allow the glue to dry.

This step is optional for both pattern based and Spoonflower based sandal construction.

 Outline sole with craft paint or tacky glue.

Sewing a Teddy Bear

Follow these steps when making the bear from a pattern. (Pattern piece 18)

 Cut out two bears from knit or felt.

Follow these steps when making the bear from Spoonflower fabric.

 If you are using the preprinted fabric from Spoonflower, cut out those pieces.

 Tip: when cutting out the front of the bear, you can make a hole by pushing a pin through the pattern to mark the position of the eyes and nose. Then use a pen to mark the positions on the fabric. Beads will be glued to these positions after stuffing.

Now follow these steps for both pattern based and Spoonflower based bear designs.

 Match the two bear pieces. The right side of the fabric should be out and the wrong sides should be touching.

 Start at one "leave open" dot and sew around the bear. End at the other dot.

 Stuff the bear through the open area.

 Sew up the stuffing opening.

 For the bear from a pattern, glue on two black 2 mm beads for the eyes and one ⅛" black bead for the nose. Tie a bow around its neck, if you like.

31

A Cat Pattern from Florabunda's Kid Page

Here is a pattern for a stuffed cat to make for your mini doll. You can download a free PDF file of this cat pattern in three sizes. Go to sherralynsdolls.com and select Florabunda's Kid's Page. You will find many sewing and craft activities. Everything on the page is free and doll related.

If you prefer, you can copy the pattern on this page with a copier or trace it. Then use the instructions for the bear on the previous page to complete the cat.

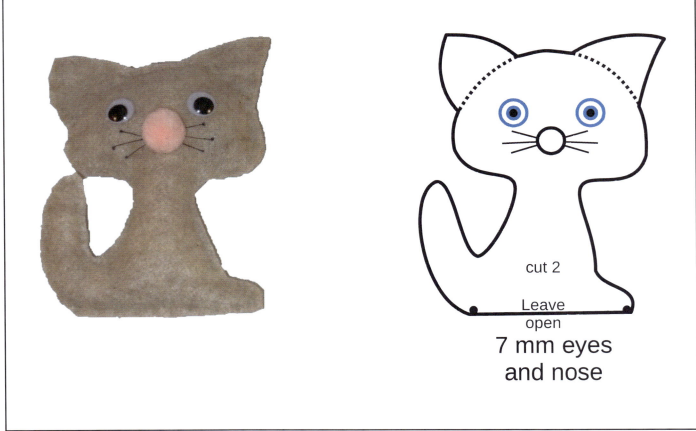

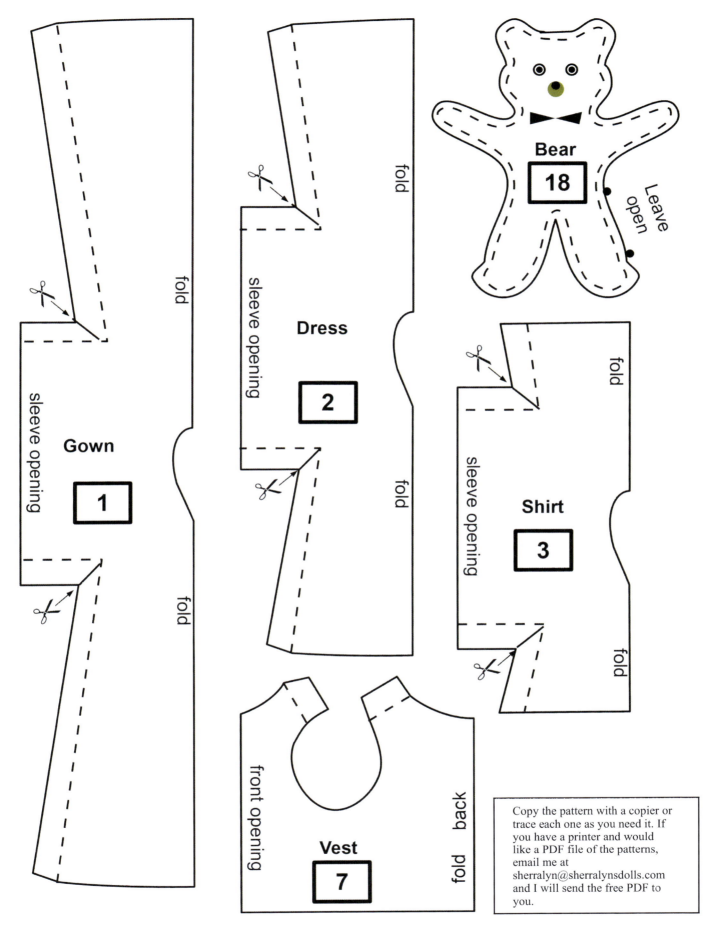

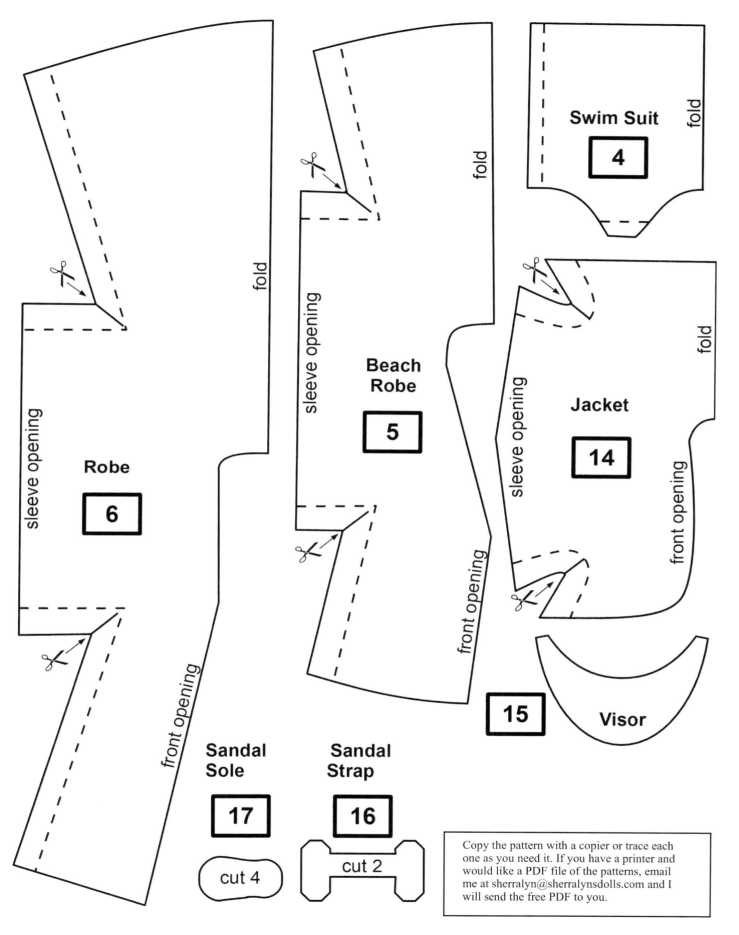

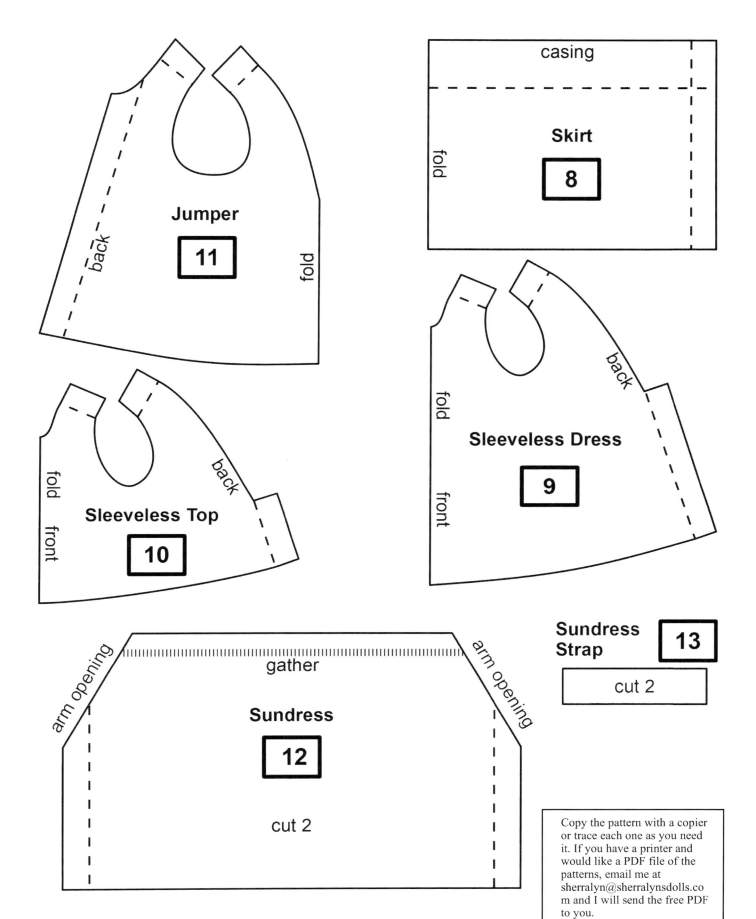

More Books

Are you ready to take the next step in sewing and learn to use the sewing machine? If so check out *Learn to Sew for your Doll*.

The book explains how to make a wardrobe for an eighteen inch doll using a sewing machine. The patterns are still easy, but they add more sewing skills to those that you learned in this book.

Attention intermediate level sewers! If you are interested in sewing for mini dolls you need my book *Sewing for Mini Dolls*. The book is filled with patterns and ideas for making a large wardrobe for a mini doll. The patterns in the book will fit 6½" American Girl® mini dolls; Our Generation® mini dolls and Lori mini dolls from Target®; and my Twinkle cloth doll. Most of the patterns will also fit Madame Alexander® Travel Friends dolls.

The book contains many styles of dresses, from plain to fancy. It has shorts, skirts, and jeans all with optional pockets; and T-shirts, sweaters, jackets, coats, and raincoats. It has nightgowns, robes, underwear, socks and tights. The accessories include, shoes, a purse, a hat, a backpack, and an umbrella. You can also make a doll bed and my 6½" (16.5 cm) cloth doll, Twinkle.

Custom Printed Fabric from Spoonflower

You can buy a fat quarter of knit from Spoonflower® that has all the clothing in this book printed on it. Just cut each piece out and sew it together. You can find a link to my Spoonflower prints on my website, sherralynsdolls.com. You can also go directly to Spoonflower's website. Use their search bar to select fabric and search for sherralynsdolls. Look through our fabric selections to find the mini doll fabric.

Printed in Great Britain
by Amazon